ANTONIO A. GORI

Surrender Novena Devotion: Powerful Prayers for Surrender to God's Will for every occasions

Contents

1	Introduction	1
2	How to Use this Book	4
3	Understanding Surrender	7
4	The Novena Devotion	14
5	How to Begin the Surrender Novena	19
6	Day 1: Surrender Novena	22
7	Day 2: Surrender Novena	25
8	Day 3: Surrender Novena	28
9	Day 4: Surrender Novena	31
10	Day 5: Surrender Novena	34
11	Day 6: Surrender Novena	37
12	Day 7: Surrender Novena	40
13	Day 8: Surrender Novena	43
14	Day 9: Surrender Novena	46
15	Prayers for Daily Surrender- Surrender for Life's Challenges	49
16	Surrender in Times of Joy and Gratitude	60
17	Surrender in Decision-Making	69
18	Surrender in Faith and Spirituality	75
19	Final Prayer of Surrender	81
20	Conclusion	83

1

Introduction

Hello and Welcome to the world of the Surrender Novena, a beautiful and simple way to connect with God. In this book, we're going to explore what surrender means and how it can bring you peace and strength. But before we dive in, let's start with some easy-to-understand basics.

What is Surrender?

Surrender is like saying, "Okay, God, I trust you." It's about letting go of the worries and struggles that weigh us down. Imagine carrying a heavy backpack filled with problems and fears. Surrendering is like taking that backpack off and handing it over to God. It's giving up control and believing that God knows what's best for us.

Why is Surrender Important?

Life can be tough, right? We face challenges, make decisions, and sometimes things don't go as planned. That's where surrender comes in. When we surrender to God, we're saying, "I can't do this on my own, God. I need your help." It's a way of finding peace in the middle of life's storms.

What's a Novena?

A novena is like a nine-day prayer journey. It's a way to connect with God over a period of time. In this book, we'll guide you through the Surrender Novena, which is made up of nine prayers. Each day, you'll pray one of these special prayers, and we'll help you understand what each one means.

This book is your companion on your surrender journey. Whether you're new to prayer or have been talking to God for a while, you'll find something here. You can use it by yourself or with friends and family. We'll explain what surrender is, why it matters, and how it can make your life better. Real people have found peace and strength through surrender, and we'll share their stories with you. These stories show that surrender is something anyone can do.

We'll guide you through the Surrender Novena, day by day. You'll find the words to say and thoughts to ponder. You don't need to be a prayer expert – just be yourself.

We'll share tips for making prayer a regular part of your life. Remember, it's not about being perfect; it's about connecting with God.

The Surrender Novena is a gift – a way to find peace, trust, and hope in your life. It's like having a conversation with God, where you can be honest about your fears and hopes. This book is here to help you on that journey, step by step, in simple language you can understand.

So, are you ready? Are you ready to let go of your worries and trust that there's something bigger than yourself? Are you ready to experience the power of surrender? Let's begin this beautiful journey together.

2

How to Use this Book

Using this book, "Surrender Novena Devotion" is easy and can become a meaningful part of your daily life. Here's a simple guide to help you get the most from it:

Start with an Open Heart: Begin by finding a quiet and comfortable place where you won't be disturbed. Take a few deep breaths and clear your mind. Approach this book with an open heart and a willingness to let go of your worries.

Read a Little Each Day: You don't need to rush through this book. It's designed for you to read a little each day, just like a daily devotion. Each day, find the section that corresponds to that day in the Novena. For example, on Day 1, read Day 1's content.

Pray the Daily Prayer: After reading the content for the day, you'll find a special prayer. This prayer is your conversation with God. Say it out loud or in your heart. You're handing over your concerns to God, like giving them to a trusted friend.

Reflect and Meditate: Take a moment to think about what you read and prayed about. How does it relate to your life? How can you apply it to your current situation? This reflection time is your chance to connect with the message on a personal level.

Live the Message: Throughout the day, try to carry the message of surrender with you. If worries or anxieties come up, remind yourself of the prayer and the idea of surrendering them to God. Trust that God is taking care of things for you.

Repeat for Nine Days: The Novena lasts for nine days, so make this a daily practice during that time. You can start on any day that feels right for you. Each day's content builds on the previous one, so it's important to follow the sequence.

Keep a Journal: Consider keeping a journal during the nine days. Write down your thoughts, feelings, and any insights that come to you. It can be a helpful way to track your progress and see how surrender is impacting your life.

Share with Others: If you feel comfortable, share your experience with friends or family. You might inspire someone else to embark on their journey of surrender, too. Sharing can also deepen your understanding and commitment to the practice.

Use Beyond the Novena: While this book is structured around the Novena, remember that surrender is a lifelong practice. You can revisit the book whenever you need guidance, whether you're facing challenges or seeking gratitude in times of joy.

Trust the Process: Above all, trust that surrendering to God's will is a process. It might not happen overnight, but with patience and faith, you'll gradually experience more peace and clarity in your life.

Remember, this book is here to support you on your spiritual journey. It's not about perfection but progress. So, take it one day at a time, one prayer at a time, and let the power of surrender work in your life.

3

Understanding Surrender

Exploring Surrender in Faith:

Surrender, in the world of faith, is like saying, "I trust you, God. I'm letting go and believing you have a plan for me." It's about giving up the idea that we always have to be in control.

Imagine you're on a roller coaster. When you're strapped in, you can't control where the ride goes. Surrendering to faith is a bit like that. It's letting go of the need to steer your life all the time and trusting that God is looking out for you.

In simpler terms, it means when life gets tough, instead of trying to solve everything by yourself, you turn to God and say, "I'm putting this in your hands." It's like sharing your worries with a caring friend who can help you through the tough times.

Surrender in faith doesn't mean you stop making decisions or taking responsibility. It means you make your choices with the belief that God's wisdom and love are guiding you. It's like having a GPS for your life, with God as the navigator.

So, exploring surrender in faith is about learning to let go of your worries, trusting in something bigger, and finding peace in knowing that you're not alone on life's journey.

The Benefits of Surrendering to God's Will:

Surrendering to God's will means saying, "Okay, God, I trust you to lead the way." When we do this, there are some really good things that happen:

Less Worry: When you surrender, you don't have to carry all your worries and problems by yourself. You hand them over to God, like giving a heavy backpack to a strong friend. This can make you feel lighter and less stressed.

More Peace: Surrendering brings a sense of calm. It's like being in a peaceful boat on a calm lake instead of a shaky boat in stormy waters. You know God's got your back, so you can relax.

Better Decisions: Trusting God's guidance can lead to better choices. It's like having a wise advisor who helps you make good decisions in life.

Stronger Faith: Surrender helps you grow in faith. You learn to trust that God's plan is better than your own. This can make your faith stronger and more resilient.

Deeper Relationships: Surrender can improve your relationships. When you let go of grudges or arguments and trust God to help, it's like putting glue on a broken friendship. It can bring people closer together.

Joy and Gratitude: Surrendering can make you happier. You start to notice the good things in life and feel grateful for them. It's like seeing a rainbow after a storm.

In a nutshell, surrendering to God's will is like handing over your worries and problems to a trusted friend. It brings peace, better decisions, and stronger faith, and it can even make your relationships better and bring more joy into your life.

Overcoming Common Misconceptions About Surrender:

Surrendering to something bigger, like God's will, can be a bit confusing sometimes. There are some common misunderstandings or misconceptions about surrender that we should clear up. Let's explore these and set the record straight in simple terms.

1. Surrender is Giving Up Control:
    - Misconception: Surrender is often thought of as giving up all control of your life, like being a puppet with no say.
    - Reality: Surrender doesn't mean you stop making choices. It's more like sharing the steering wheel of your life with someone you trust. You still drive, but you have a co-pilot (God) helping with directions.

2. Surrender Means Being Passive:
    - Misconception: Some people think surrender means sitting around and doing nothing, waiting for things to magically fall into place.
    - Reality: Surrender is about taking action with trust in God.

It's like working hard on a project while knowing that God is your backup, ensuring things work out as they should.

3. It's Only for Really Religious People:

- Misconception: Surrender is often seen as something only super-religious folks do, not for regular people.

- Reality: Surrender is for everyone, regardless of how religious you are. It's about finding peace and guidance in a chaotic world. It's like an umbrella that keeps you dry in life's storms, no matter who you are.

4. Surrender is a One-Time Thing:

- Misconception: Some think surrender is a one-and-done deal, like a contract you sign once.

- Reality: Surrender is a daily practice, not a one-time event. It's like brushing your teeth to keep them healthy. You do it regularly to maintain your spiritual well-being.

5. You Lose Your Identity:

- Misconception: People worry that if they surrender, they'll lose their unique identity and become like everyone else.

- Reality: Surrender actually helps you discover your true self. It's like cleaning a dusty mirror to see your reflection more clearly. You become more 'you' through surrender.

6. Surrender Solves Everything Instantly:

- Misconception: Some think that once they surrender, all their problems will disappear immediately.

- Reality: Surrender doesn't work like a magic wand. It's more like planting a seed. You need to nurture it over time before you see the beautiful flowers.

10

7. You Can't Feel Emotions:

  - Misconception: People fear that surrender means they can't feel emotions or express themselves.

  - Reality: Surrender allows you to feel emotions even more deeply. It's like opening a window to let fresh air in, helping you process feelings in a healthier way.

In essence, surrender isn't about giving up control or being passive. It's a practice for everyone, not just the super-religious. It's a daily habit, not a one-time thing. You don't lose yourself; you find your true identity. It's not instant magic but a gradual process. And it doesn't make you emotionless; it helps you connect with your feelings in a more meaningful way. Under-standing these truths about surrender can help you embrace it as a valuable tool for navigating life's journey.

Practical tips for integrating Surrender into your daily routine

Integrating surrender into your daily routine can lead to a more peaceful and spiritually fulfilling life. Below are some practical tips to help you make surrender a part of your daily life:

1. Morning Prayer: Start your day with a prayer of surrender. Offer your day to God, asking for guidance and strength to trust in His will. This sets a positive tone for the day.

2. Pause and Breathe: Throughout the day, take short breaks to pause and breathe deeply. Use these moments to surrender any worries or stresses to God. Imagine exhaling your concerns with each breath.

3. Mindfulness and Meditation: Practice mindfulness or med-

itation to become more aware of your thoughts and emotions.
When you notice anxiety or resistance, surrender those feelings
to God's care.

4. Gratitude Journal: Maintain a gratitude journal to remind
yourself of the blessings in your life. Recognizing and appreci-
ating these gifts can help you trust in God's providence.

5. Let Go of Control: Recognize when you're trying to control
situations beyond your power. Remind yourself that surrender
means letting go and trusting that God is in control.

6. Trust in Divine Timing: When things don't go as planned,
trust that there's a reason. Embrace the idea that God's timing
is often different from yours and that His plan is always for your
best.

7. Relinquish Resentment: Practice forgiveness and let go of
grudges. Forgiving others and yourself is a powerful act of
surrender that brings emotional freedom.

8. Prayer Throughout the Day: Incorporate short prayers of
surrender into your daily activities. For example, when you're
stuck in traffic or facing a challenging task, silently offer it to
God.

9. Seek Guidance: When faced with major decisions, seek God's
guidance through prayer and reflection. Trust that He will lead
you in the right direction.

10. Evening Reflection: Before bed, reflect on your day. Acknowl-

edge moments of surrender and areas where you struggled. Use this time to offer gratitude for the day's experiences, both positive and challenging.

11. Community and Support: Surround yourself with a supportive community of faith. Sharing your journey of surrender with others can provide encouragement and accountability.

12. Practice Patience: Understand that surrender is a process. Be patient with yourself as you learn to let go and trust. It's okay to stumble; what matters is your willingness to keep trying.

13. Stay Grounded in Scripture: Read and meditate on Scripture passages that emphasize trust and surrender. The Bible offers valuable guidance and inspiration.

14. Spiritual Retreats: Consider participating in retreats or workshops focused on surrender and spiritual growth. These experiences can deepen your understanding and practice.

15. Daily Affirmations: Create positive affirmations that reinforce surrender and trust. Repeat these affirmations daily to reprogram your thought patterns.

Remember that integrating surrender into your daily routine is a journey, not an instant transformation. Be gentle with yourself, and trust that over time, this practice will bring greater peace and alignment with God's will in your life.

4

The Novena Devotion

A novena is like a special nine-day prayer adventure. It's a way to talk to God and build a deeper connection with Him. Let's break down what a novena is and how it works in simple terms:

What's a Novena?
   - A novena is a series of prayers you say for nine days in a row. It's like having a daily chat with God.

The Structure of a Novena:
   - Each day of the novena, you say a specific prayer or set of prayers. These prayers often have a particular theme or focus.
   - Novenas usually have a goal or intention. This means you're praying for something specific, like guidance, healing, or peace.
   - Some novenas involve saying the same prayer each day, while others have different prayers for each day. It depends on the novena's design.

Daily Prayers:
   - During a novena, you have a little "prayer plan" for each

day. It's like following a recipe.

- You might start with a special opening prayer, like saying "Hi" to God.

- Then, there could be a series of prayers or reflections that help you focus on your intention.

- At the end of the day's prayers, you might finish with a closing prayer, like saying "Goodnight" to God.

Reflecting and Asking:

- While saying the prayers, you also think about your intention. This is like telling God what's on your mind and heart.

- You might ask God for help, guidance, or whatever you need. It's like having a friendly conversation with Him.

Consistency is Key:

- Novenas are designed to be done every day for nine days. It's a bit like watering a plant every day – it helps your connection with God grow.

Why Nine Days?

- Nine is a special number in many cultures and religions. It's often associated with completion or fulfillment. So, after nine days of praying, you might feel a sense of fulfillment or a deeper connection with God.

What's the Point?

- The goal of a novena is to bring you closer to God and to help you with your intention. It's like asking a trusted friend for support.

Remember, novenas are a way to express your feelings, hopes,

and needs to God. They're a bit like a heartfelt letter to a friend.
By following the prayers and reflecting each day, you're creating
a space for God to listen and respond in His own way.

So, that's the structure of a novena – a nine-day journey of
prayer and reflection that can bring you closer to God and
help you with whatever you're facing in life. It's a simple yet
powerful way to connect with the divine.

How the Novena aligns with Catholic Teachings and

Let's break down how the novena aligns with Catholic teachings and tradition in simple terms:

1. Daily Prayer: Novenas involve daily prayers, and prayer is a
fundamental part of Catholic tradition. Catholics believe that
through prayer, they can communicate with God, seek guidance,
and build a deeper relationship with Him. So, when you do a
novena, you're following this Catholic practice of regular prayer.

2. Intention: In a novena, you have a specific intention or goal
for your prayers. This aligns with Catholic teachings because
Catholics are encouraged to pray with purpose. It's like having
a heartfelt request when talking to God, which is a common
Catholic practice.

3. Repetition: Some novenas involve saying the same prayer or
set of prayers each day for nine days. Repetition in prayer is a
way to focus your thoughts and intentions, and it's a technique
used in Catholic spirituality to deepen one's connection with
God.

4. Faith and Trust: The act of doing a novena demonstrates faith and trust in God's response. Catholics believe that God listens to their prayers and answers them in His way and time. By committing to the novena for nine days, you're showing your trust in God's plan, another core Catholic belief.

5. Seeking Intercession: Many novenas involve asking for the intercession of a saint or a holy figure. In Catholic tradition, saints are seen as close friends of God who can help intercede on your behalf. So, when you include a saint's intercession in your novena, you're following a well-established Catholic practice.

6. Reflecting on Scripture: Some novenas include reflections on passages from the Bible. The Bible holds immense importance in Catholic teachings, and reflecting on its teachings during a novena helps Catholics connect their prayers to sacred scripture.

7. Tradition of Nine Days: The nine-day duration of a novena carries special significance in Catholic tradition. It is often associated with waiting and preparing for something important. For example, the original novena in Catholic history was the nine days that the apostles spent in prayer between Jesus' Ascension and the coming of the Holy Spirit at Pentecost. So, the nine days in a novena have historical and symbolic meaning.

In summary, the novena aligns with Catholic teachings and tradition by incorporating daily prayer, specific intentions, repetition, faith, intercession of saints, reflection on scripture, and the use of a nine-day period. It's a way for Catholics to deepen their relationship with God, seek His guidance, and express their faith and trust in His divine plan in a structured and meaningful manner.

5

How to Begin the Surrender Novena

Praying the Surrender Novena is a beautiful and simple process. Below are step-by-step instructions in easy-to-understand terms:

Step 1: Prepare Your Space

- Find a quiet, comfortable place where you won't be disturbed. It could be your bedroom, a cozy chair, or even a peaceful spot outside.

Step 2: Set Your Intention

- Think about what you want to surrender or ask for guidance on. It could be a problem you're facing, a decision you need to make, or simply a desire for peace. This is your "intention."

Step 3: Day 1 Prayer

- On the first day of the novena, start by saying a simple opening prayer. You can use your own words or this one: "Dear God, I come to you with an open heart, ready to surrender my intentions to your will."

Step 4: Day-Specific Prayer

- Each day of the novena, you'll say a special prayer specific to that day. You can find these prayers in a prayer book or online. They are usually written out for you to follow.

Step 5: Reflect and Talk to God

- After saying the day's prayer, take a few moments to think about your intention. Talk to God like you would talk to a friend. Tell Him what's on your mind and in your heart. Be honest and sincere.

Step 6: Day 1 Closing Prayer

- Finish the first day by saying a closing prayer. You can say something like, "God, I trust that you hear my prayers. Help me to surrender to your will and find peace."

Step 7: Repeat for Nine Days

- Repeat Steps 3 to 6 for the next eight days, using the specific prayer for each day. Remember to keep your intention in mind as you pray.

Step 8: Reflect on Your Journey

- After the ninth day, take some time to reflect on your novena journey. How do you feel? Have you found more peace or clarity? What did you learn about surrender?

Step 9: Trust God's Timing

- Understand that God may answer your prayer in His own time and in a way that's best for you, even if it's not exactly what you expected. Trust in His wisdom.

Step 10: Continue Your Relationship with God

- Praying the Surrender Novena isn't a one-time thing. It's a way to deepen your relationship with God. Continue to pray and talk to Him regularly, knowing that He's always there for you.

Remember, there's no right or wrong way to pray the Surrender Novena. It's about opening your heart to God, surrendering your worries or desires to His care, and trusting that He will guide you on your journey.

6

Day 1: Surrender Novena

Opening Prayer

Dear Heavenly Father,

As we embark on this nine-day journey of surrender, we come before you with open hearts and eager spirits. We seek your guidance, your love, and your strength to help us let go of our worries and trust in your divine plan. You are the author of our lives, and we surrender our stories to your wisdom.

Lord, in this moment, we bring to you our deepest concerns, the burdens that weigh heavy on our hearts. We offer them up to you, knowing that your love is greater than any challenge we face. Please grant us the grace to release our anxieties and to embrace the peace that comes from surrendering to your will.

As we reflect on this first day, help us remember that surrender is not a sign of weakness but an act of courage. It takes strength to place our trust in your hands and relinquish control. In our surrender, we find freedom and hope.

Day 1: Reflection

Take a moment to consider the burdens you carry, the worries that keep you up at night. Imagine them as heavy stones in your backpack, weighing you down. Now, envision placing these stones one by one into the hands of God. As you do, feel the lightness and relief that comes with surrender.

Surrendering can be scary because it means admitting that we don't have all the answers. But it also means acknowledging that God does, and that's a comforting thought. Surrender opens the door to divine guidance and support.

Prayer

Heavenly Father,

Today, we surrender our worries and fears to you. We release the weight of our burdens and place our trust in your loving care. We know that you see our struggles, and you are with us every step of the way.

Lord, grant us the strength to continue this journey of surrender. Help us to remember that your plan for our lives is greater than anything we could ever imagine. May we find peace in the knowledge that we are not alone, for you are our ever-present companion.

In your name, we pray. Amen.

As we conclude this first day of our Surrender Novena, may you carry the peace of surrender with you. Know that God is with you, guiding your steps, and lightening your load as you continue this journey of faith and trust.

7

Day 2: Surrender Novena

Opening Prayer

Heavenly Father,

As we gather on this second day of our Surrender Novena, we come before you with hearts full of gratitude for guiding us through the first day of surrender. We thank you for your unwavering love and support. Today, we continue this journey, placing our trust in your divine plan.

Lord, we bring before you the challenges and uncertainties that lie ahead. We acknowledge that we do not have all the answers, but we trust that you hold the key to our future. Help us to surrender our desires and fears, knowing that your will is always for our highest good.

As we embark on this day of reflection, open our hearts to the wisdom that comes from surrender. Teach us to let go of our need for control and to embrace the peace that can only be found in you.

Day 2: Reflection

Take a moment to reflect on the things you've been trying to control in your life. Maybe it's a relationship, a career, or a health concern. Consider how holding on tightly to these things has affected you emotionally and spiritually. Now, imagine releasing them into God's hands. Picture the freedom and relief that surrender can bring.

Surrender is not about giving up; it's about gaining a deeper connection with God. When we let go of our need to control every aspect of our lives, we make room for God's divine guidance and blessings to flow in.

Prayer

Dear Lord,

On this second day of our Surrender Novena, we lay before you our desires and ambitions. We surrender our plans and dreams, knowing that your plans for us are far greater than we can imagine.

Help us to trust in your timing, even when it doesn't align with our own. Grant us the patience to wait for your perfect plan to unfold. In moments of doubt, remind us that you are always by our side, guiding us with love.

We surrender, Lord, and we do so with open hearts, ready to

receive your blessings. May our faith deepen with each passing day of this novena.

In your holy name, we pray. Amen.

As we conclude this second day of our Surrender Novena, may you find comfort in surrendering your desires to God. Know that in letting go, you open yourself up to divine possibilities and a deeper connection with the One who knows what's best for you.

8

Day 3: Surrender Novena

Opening Prayer

Gracious God,

On this third day of our Surrender Novena, we come before you with hearts filled with hope and trust. We thank you for guiding us through the journey of surrender thus far and for the peace that is slowly settling into our souls. As we continue, help us to deepen our surrender and strengthen our faith.

Lord, we carry with us the challenges and uncertainties of our lives. We lay them at your feet, knowing that you are the ultimate source of wisdom and love. Teach us to surrender not just our worries but also our desires, that we may align ourselves more closely with your divine will.

As we embark on this day's reflection, may we find solace in your presence and the courage to surrender even more completely.

Day 3: Reflection

Consider the times in your life when you've felt most at peace. Was it when you were in control of everything, or was it when you let go and trusted in something greater than yourself? Think about the relief that comes from surrendering your burdens and desires. Reflect on how surrender can be a path to inner serenity.

Surrender isn't about giving up on your dreams; it's about allowing them to unfold in the way that's best for you. It's like planting seeds in a garden and trusting that they will grow into beautiful flowers with time.

Prayer

Heavenly Father,

On this third day of our Surrender Novena, we surrender our dreams and ambitions to you. We recognize that your plans for us are filled with love and purpose. Help us to release our need for control and embrace the beauty of surrender.

Lord, we trust that you know the desires of our hearts better than we do. May our surrender be an act of faith, believing that your way is always the best way, even when we can't see the full picture.

Grant us the grace to remain patient and steadfast in our surrender, knowing that you are with us every step of the way.

In your name, we pray. Amen.

As we conclude this third day of our Surrender Novena, may you find peace in surrendering your dreams to the loving hands of God. Know that in letting go, you make space for God's divine plan to unfold, bringing you closer to the fulfillment of your heart's desires.

9

Day 4: Surrender Novena

Opening Prayer

Dear Heavenly Father,

As we gather on this fourth day of our Surrender Novena, we approach you with grateful hearts for the strength and guidance you've provided throughout this journey of surrender. We are learning to release our grip on control and place our trust in your divine plan.

Lord, today, we bring before you the struggles and challenges that have weighed on our hearts. We surrender them to you, knowing that your love and wisdom are greater than any obstacle we face. Open our hearts to receive the peace that comes from relinquishing our fears and worries into your capable hands.

As we delve into today's reflection, may we find solace and inspiration to continue surrendering with even greater trust.

Day 4: Reflection

Take a moment to reflect on the times in your life when you've faced adversity. How did you handle those challenges? Did you try to control every aspect, or did you turn to God for guidance and strength? Consider the peace that can come from surrendering your difficulties to a higher power.

Surrender is like turning to a loving parent when you're lost in a big, unfamiliar place. You let go of the fear of being alone and trust that you'll be taken care of. Surrendering your challenges to God is similar; you're letting go of fear and embracing trust.

Prayer

Heavenly Father,

On this fourth day of our Surrender Novena, we surrender our struggles and challenges to you. We trust that your plan for us is filled with purpose, even in the midst of difficulties. Help us to let go of the need to control every aspect of our lives and find peace in surrender.

Lord, we ask for the strength to persevere in the face of adversity. Grant us the wisdom to see the lessons in our challenges and the faith to trust that you are guiding us toward a brighter future.

In our surrender, may we find the grace to endure and the hope to keep moving forward, knowing that you walk with us every step of the way.

In your loving name, we pray. Amen.

As we conclude this fourth day of our Surrender Novena, may you find comfort in surrendering your struggles to God. Trust that in letting go, you make room for divine support and guidance to help you navigate the challenges that lie ahead.

10

Day 5: Surrender Novena

Opening Prayer

Loving God,

On this fifth day of our Surrender Novena, we come before you with hearts brimming with gratitude for the journey you've led us on thus far. We thank you for the peace and strength that surrender is bringing into our lives. As we continue, help us deepen our trust in your divine plan.

Lord, today we bring before you our relationships—the bonds of family, friends, and loved ones. We surrender them to your loving care, knowing that you are the ultimate source of love and reconciliation. Teach us to release our hurts, fears, and conflicts into your hands, that we may experience the healing power of surrender.

As we embark on this day's reflection, may we find solace in your presence and the courage to surrender our relationships with open hearts.

Day 5: Reflection

Take a moment to reflect on the relationships in your life. Consider any conflicts, misunderstandings, or hurts that may have strained these bonds. Now, imagine releasing these burdens and placing them in God's hands, as if lifting a heavy weight from your shoulders. Think about the freedom and healing that surrender can bring to your relationships.

Surrender in relationships is like extending an olive branch. It's a gesture of peace and trust, allowing God to work in the hearts of both parties, bringing understanding and reconciliation.

Prayer

Dear Lord,

On this fifth day of our Surrender Novena, we surrender our relationships to you. We lay before you the joys and the challenges, the love and the conflicts, trusting that your love is greater than any division.

Lord, we ask for the grace to forgive and to seek forgiveness, to love and to be loved, just as you have loved us. We surrender our desires for reconciliation, trusting that your healing touch can mend what is broken.

In our surrender, may we find the strength to extend grace and understanding, just as you have extended them to us.

In your name, we pray. Amen.

As we conclude this fifth day of our Surrender Novena, may you find hope and healing in surrendering your relationships to God. Trust that in letting go, you make space for divine love and reconciliation to work wonders in your connections with others.

11

Day 6: Surrender Novena

Opening Prayer

Heavenly Father,

As we gather on this sixth day of our Surrender Novena, our hearts are filled with gratitude for the journey you've led us on. We are learning the beauty of surrendering to your divine plan and the peace it brings into our lives. Today, we come to you with our fears and anxieties.

Lord, we surrender our worries and fears into your loving hands, knowing that your love casts out all fear. As we embark on this day's reflection, open our hearts to the calm that comes from releasing our anxieties and embracing trust in your perfect plan.

In this moment, help us to let go and let you take the reins of our lives, for we know your ways are always filled with love and purpose.

Day 6: Reflection

Take a moment to reflect on the fears and anxieties that have
been weighing on your heart. These fears may be about your
future, your health, your family, or any other aspect of life. Now,
imagine releasing these fears into God's loving hands, as if
setting down a heavy burden. Consider the peace that surrender
can bring when you trust in God's protective care.

Surrendering your fears is like seeking shelter in a loving
embrace during a storm. It's trusting that God will shield you
from life's turbulence, providing a sense of security and peace.

Prayer

Dear Lord,

On this sixth day of our Surrender Novena, we come before you
with our fears and anxieties. We acknowledge that, at times, our
worries can overwhelm us. Today, we choose to surrender them
to you.

Lord, help us to trust in your providence, even when we cannot
see the way ahead. Grant us the courage to face our fears with the
knowledge that you are with us, guiding us through the darkest
moments.

In our surrender, may we find the peace that surpasses all
understanding and the strength to walk confidently, knowing
that you are our protector and our refuge.

In your holy name, we pray. Amen.

As we conclude this sixth day of our Surrender Novena, may you find solace in surrendering your fears to God. Trust that in letting go, you create space for divine comfort and courage to fill your heart, guiding you through life's uncertainties with unwavering faith.

12

Day 7: Surrender Novena

Opening Prayer

Loving and Gracious God,

As we gather on this seventh day of our Surrender Novena, we approach you with hearts overflowing with gratitude for the journey we've undertaken. We thank you for the peace and strength that surrender is bringing into our lives. Today, we bring before you our hopes and dreams.

Lord, we surrender our dreams and aspirations into your loving care, knowing that your plan for us is greater than anything we could imagine. We open our hearts to your divine guidance, trusting that you will lead us to the fulfillment of our deepest desires.

As we embark on this day's reflection, may you inspire us to surrender our dreams with unwavering faith and open hearts.

Day 7: Reflection

Take a moment to reflect on your dreams and aspirations. What are the things you've longed for in life? Imagine these dreams as beautiful balloons that you're releasing into the sky, one by one. Consider the freedom and joy that surrender can bring when you trust in God's plan for your future.

Surrendering your dreams is like planting seeds in fertile soil. You trust that God's hands will nurture them, and in due time, they will bloom into something even more beautiful than you envisioned.

Prayer

Dear Heavenly Father,

On this seventh day of our Surrender Novena, we lay before you our hopes and dreams. We surrender them to your divine will, knowing that your plan for us is filled with purpose and love.

Lord, we ask for the grace to trust in your timing, even when it doesn't align with our own. Grant us the patience to wait for your perfect plan to unfold, and the faith to believe that your way is always the best way.

In our surrender, may we find the courage to pursue our dreams with unwavering hope, knowing that you walk alongside us on this journey.

In your holy name, we pray. Amen.

As we conclude this seventh day of our Surrender Novena, may you find peace in surrendering your dreams to God. Trust that in letting go, you make space for divine guidance and blessings to lead you toward the fulfillment of your heart's desires.

13

Day 8: Surrender Novena

Opening Prayer

Gracious God,

As we gather on this eighth day of our Surrender Novena, we come before you with hearts filled with awe and gratitude for the transformative journey we've experienced. We thank you for the peace and strength that surrender has brought into our lives. Today, we lay before you our failures and shortcomings.

Lord, we surrender our mistakes, our flaws, and our past regrets into your loving hands, knowing that your forgiveness is boundless. Teach us to release the weight of guilt and shame, that we may find healing and restoration through surrender.

As we embark on this day's reflection, may you inspire us to let go of the burdens of our past and embrace the freedom that comes from your mercy.

Day 8: Reflection

Take a moment to reflect on the mistakes and failures you carry in your heart. Consider the times you've fallen short or hurt others. Now, imagine placing these burdens at the foot of the cross, where God's forgiveness and grace flow freely. Think about the lightness and peace that surrendering your past can bring.

Surrendering your mistakes is like stepping out of the shadows and into the warm embrace of God's love. It's acknowledging that, despite your imperfections, you are worthy of divine mercy and healing.

Prayer

Heavenly Father,

On this eighth day of our Surrender Novena, we surrender our failures and shortcomings to you. We lay before you the mistakes we've made and the regrets that weigh on our hearts.

Lord, we ask for the gift of your forgiveness and the grace to forgive ourselves. Help us to let go of the past and embrace the new beginnings that your mercy offers. May our surrender be an act of trust in your infinite love and your power to redeem.

In our surrender, may we find the freedom to live without the heavy chains of guilt and shame, knowing that your love restores and heals.

In your name, we pray. Amen.

As we conclude this eighth day of our Surrender Novena, may you find solace in surrendering your past mistakes to God. Trust that in letting go, you make space for divine forgiveness and restoration to bring light and healing to your soul.

14

Day 9: Surrender Novena

Opening Prayer

Dear Heavenly Father,

As we gather on this ninth and final day of our Surrender Novena, our hearts are overflowing with gratitude for the incredible journey of transformation we've experienced. We thank you for the peace and strength that surrender has brought into our lives. Today, we come before you with our future.

Lord, we surrender our dreams and plans for the future into your loving hands, knowing that your divine plan is greater than anything we could imagine. Teach us to release our anxieties about what lies ahead and trust that you hold the future in your capable hands.

As we embark on this day's reflection, may you inspire us to surrender our futures with unwavering faith, knowing that you are our guiding light.

Day 9: Reflection

Take a moment to reflect on the uncertainties and anxieties you may have about the future. Consider the paths you hope to follow and the dreams you hold dear. Now, imagine entrusting these aspirations to God's care, like placing them in a treasure chest and sealing it with trust. Think about the peace and hope that surrendering your future can bring.

Surrendering your future is like handing over the map of your life to a loving guide. It's knowing that God's plan is the best route, even when you can't see all the turns and detours ahead.

Prayer

Loving Father,

On this ninth and final day of our Surrender Novena, we lay before you our hopes and dreams for the future. We surrender them to your divine will, knowing that your plan for us is filled with love and purpose.

Lord, help us to trust in your timing, even when it doesn't align with our own. Grant us the courage to embrace the unknown, knowing that you are the light that guides our path.

In our surrender, may we find the peace that comes from placing our trust in you, the author of our future.

In your holy name, we pray. Amen.

As we conclude this ninth day of our Surrender Novena, may you find peace and hope in surrendering your future to God. Trust that in letting go, you create space for divine guidance and blessings to lead you toward the fulfillment of your heart's desires on the beautiful journey ahead.

15

Prayers for Daily Surrender- Surrender for Life's Challenges

A guide with prayers and guidance for surrendering during times of hardship, grief, and uncertainty:

Prayer of Surrender:

Dear Heavenly Father,

In this season of hardship, grief, and uncertainty, I come before you with a heart weighed down by the burdens of life's challenges. I acknowledge that, in my humanity, I cannot control the circumstances that surround me. But I trust in your divine sovereignty, knowing that you hold all things in your capable hands.

Today, I surrender to you. I surrender my worries, my fears, and my pain. I lay them at the foot of your throne, knowing that your love is greater than any trial I face. Help me, dear Lord, to release the need for control and to trust wholly in your perfect plan.

Grant me the strength to endure the storms that rage around me. Infuse me with the wisdom to discern your purpose in this season of my life. May I have the faith to understand that you are with me, even in the darkest moments, guiding me through each trial.

May your peace, which surpasses all understanding, fill my heart and mind. May your light illuminate my path, even when it seems obscured by the shadows of uncertainty.

In your holy and loving name, I surrender.

Guidance for Surrender:

1. Acknowledge Your Feelings:
   - During challenging times, it's essential to acknowledge and honor your feelings. Allow yourself to grieve, feel anger, or experience sadness. Surrender doesn't mean suppressing your emotions; it means entrusting them to God's care. Take time to process and express what you're going through.

2. Prayer and Meditation:
   - Set aside time for prayer and meditation. These practices can help you connect with God, find solace, and gain perspective. In prayer, express your thoughts, feelings, and concerns honestly. Meditate on Scripture passages that offer comfort and hope.

3. Release Control:
   - Surrender often involves letting go of the illusion of control.

Understand that there are aspects of life you cannot change, but you can choose how you respond to them. Give up the need to control every outcome, and trust in God's sovereign plan.

4. Trust in God's Character:
    - In moments of hardship, remind yourself of God's attributes. Reflect on His love, mercy, and faithfulness. Trust that God is working for your good, even when you can't see it. Hold onto the belief that He is a loving and caring Father.

5. Community and Support:
    - Lean on your faith community, friends, and family for support. Sharing your burdens with others can lighten the load and offer comfort. Don't hesitate to seek companionship and encouragement during difficult times.

6. Practice Gratitude:
    - Even amidst hardship, find things to be grateful for. Practicing gratitude can shift your perspective and open your heart to surrender. It helps you focus on the positive aspects of your life, no matter how small they may seem.

7. Journaling:
    - Keeping a journal can be a therapeutic way to navigate your emotions and your journey of surrender. Write down your thoughts, prayers, and reflections. Document your experiences and track your progress as you learn to surrender.

8. Let Go of Blame:
    - Release blame and self-criticism. Understand that surrender involves forgiving yourself and others for mistakes and short-

comings. Forgiveness is a powerful act of surrender that can bring emotional healing.

9. Seek Guidance:

- If you find it challenging to navigate your feelings of grief and uncertainty, seek guidance from a spiritual leader, counselor, or therapist. They can provide professional support and help you find clarity during difficult times.

10. Daily Surrender:

- Make surrender a daily practice. Each morning, offer your day to God through prayer. Ask for His guidance, strength, and presence throughout the day. Each night, release the day's worries and uncertainties into His loving hands, trusting that He watches over you as you sleep.

11. Hold onto Hope:

- Remember that, even in the darkest times, there is hope. Surrender is an act of faith that allows God's light to shine through your difficulties. Hold onto the belief that, through surrender, you can find strength, peace, and a deeper connection with God, even amidst hardship and uncertainty.

12. Embrace Vulnerability:

- Surrender often involves embracing vulnerability. Understand that it's okay to feel fragile and exposed during challenging times. Surrendering your need to appear strong allows you to receive the support and comfort you need from God and others.

13. Revisit Your Faith:

- Use difficult times as an opportunity to deepen your faith.

Revisit your spiritual beliefs and practices. Seek to grow in your understanding of God's love and His plan for your life. Reading spiritual literature and engaging in conversations with spiritual mentors can help in this process.

14. Trust the Process:
   - Surrender is a journey, not a destination. Understand that it's normal to have moments of struggle and doubt. Trust the process of surrender, and be patient with yourself. Continue to surrender daily, and over time, you will find increased peace and strength.

15. Seek Professional Help When Needed:
   - If you are struggling with grief or uncertainty to the point where it is severely impacting your mental and emotional well-being, consider seeking professional help from a counselor or therapist. They can provide specific tools and strategies to help you cope with these challenges.

In times of hardship, grief, and uncertainty, surrender is not a sign of weakness but an act of faith and trust in a higher power. It is through surrender that you can find strength, peace, and resilience to navigate life's most difficult moments. Remember that you are not alone in your journey, and God is with you every step of the way, offering His love, comfort, and guidance.
Prayers for health, financial struggles, and relationship challenges:

Prayer for Health:

Heavenly Father,

I come before you with a heart heavy with concern for my health. You, who are the Great Physician, I surrender my body, my mind, and my spirit into your loving care.

Please, Lord, grant me the strength and courage to face my health challenges with grace and resilience. Be my healer, guiding the hands of medical professionals, and working miracles where it is needed.

I ask for wisdom to make the right choices regarding my health, whether it be in treatment options, lifestyle changes, or seeking help from those who can provide it. Give me the patience to endure, the faith to believe in your healing power, and the hope to see a brighter, healthier future.

I surrender my anxiety, fear, and uncertainty about my health. Replace them with your peace, assurance, and trust that you are in control. Teach me to find joy and gratitude in every moment, despite my physical condition.

May my health struggles draw me closer to you, deepen my faith, and inspire me to be a source of encouragement and support for others facing similar challenges.

In your mighty and healing name, I pray. Amen.

Prayer for Financial Struggles:

Heavenly Provider,

In the midst of my financial struggles, I come to you with an open heart and a humble spirit. I surrender my financial worries and burdens into your capable hands.

Lord, you are the source of all abundance, and I trust that you will meet my needs according to your glorious riches. Please grant me the wisdom to manage my finances wisely and the discipline to make sound financial decisions.

Help me to see opportunities for growth and prosperity even in the midst of financial difficulty. Provide me with the resources and assistance I need to overcome these challenges.

I surrender the fear and anxiety that often accompany financial struggles. Replace them with faith and confidence in your provision. Teach me to be a good steward of the resources you entrust to me.

May this time of financial hardship draw me closer to you, deepen my reliance on your grace, and inspire me to be a compassionate helper to others facing financial challenges.

In your name, the name of the Great Provider, I pray. Amen.

Prayer for Relationship Challenges:

Loving God,

I bring before you the challenges in my relationships that weigh heavy on my heart. I surrender these difficulties to your divine care.

Lord, you are the great reconciler, and I ask for your guidance and wisdom to navigate these troubled waters. Grant me the patience to listen and the courage to communicate honestly and lovingly.

Help me to release any bitterness, anger, or resentment I may be holding onto, and replace these emotions with forgiveness, compassion, and empathy. Teach me to see others through your eyes and to love as you love.

I surrender the need to control or fix these relationships. I trust that you are at work in them, even when I cannot see it. May your healing touch mend what is broken and restore what is lost.

Give me the strength to set healthy boundaries, to seek reconciliation where possible, and to let go when necessary. Help me to release the outcome into your loving hands, knowing that your plan is always for our highest good.

May this time of relationship challenges draw me closer to you, deepen my capacity for love and forgiveness, and inspire me to be a peacemaker and a source of healing in the lives of those I love.

In your name, the name of the God of love, I pray. Amen.

In times of health struggles, financial difficulties, or relationship challenges, surrendering to God can bring comfort, guidance, and strength. These prayers are offered as a source of solace and hope, reminding us that we are never alone in our trials, and that God is always with us, ready to provide healing, provision, and reconciliation according to His perfect plan. Inspiring stories of individuals who found strength through surrender during tough times:

Sarah's Battle with Cancer

Sarah had always been a vibrant, active woman. She loved hiking, dancing, and spending time with her family. However, her life took an unexpected turn when she was diagnosed with a rare and aggressive form of cancer.

The news was devastating, and Sarah's initial response was fear and anger. She couldn't understand why this was happening to her. But as she began her treatment journey, something remarkable happened.

Sarah turned to her faith and decided to surrender her fears and anxieties to God. She realized that she couldn't control the outcome of her illness, but she could control how she faced it. She prayed for strength and peace, not knowing what the future held.

As the days turned into weeks and months of treatments, Sarah's surrender deepened. She learned to let go of her need to plan every aspect of her life and trust that God had a plan for her, even in the midst of suffering.

Through this surrender, Sarah found a profound sense of inner peace. She became an inspiration to others at the cancer center, always offering a listening ear and words of encouragement. She embraced each day as a gift, cherishing the moments with her loved ones.

Despite the physical and emotional challenges, Sarah's surrender allowed her to find strength she never knew she had. Her journey became a testament to the power of faith and surrender in the face of adversity. While her battle with cancer was not without its difficulties, it was marked by a deep and abiding sense of peace that carried her through.

Mark's Financial Crisis

Mark had always been a successful entrepreneur. He built a thriving business from the ground up, providing well for his family and enjoying the fruits of his labor. However, the economic downturn of 2008 hit his industry hard, and his business began to crumble.

As debts mounted, Mark found himself facing a financial crisis that seemed insurmountable. He tried everything to save his business, from cutting costs to seeking new investors, but nothing seemed to work. The stress and anxiety weighed heavily on him and his family.

One day, feeling defeated and desperate, Mark sat down in his empty office and began to pray. He surrendered his business, his financial worries, and his pride to God. He realized that he couldn't control the economy or the outcome of his efforts. He needed to trust in something greater.

Through his surrender, Mark experienced a profound shift in perspective. He began to focus on what truly mattered—his family, his health, and his faith. He downsized his lifestyle and started exploring new career opportunities outside his struggling industry.

Over time, Mark's surrender led him to discover a new path—one he would have never considered if not for his financial crisis. He found a sense of purpose in helping others facing similar challenges and became involved in financial counseling and coaching.

While Mark's financial crisis was undoubtedly a difficult chapter in his life, it became a turning point. His surrender allowed him to find strength in vulnerability and humility. He rebuilt his life on a foundation of faith, family, and service to others. Today, he looks back on that challenging time as a period of transformation and renewal.

These stories illustrate the power of surrender in the face of adversity. In times of struggle, surrender can lead to unexpected sources of strength, resilience, and growth. It reminds us that we are not alone in our challenges and that there is hope and grace in surrendering to a higher power.

16

Surrender in Times of Joy and Gratitude

Prayers and meditations for expressing gratitude and surrendering in moments of joy and success:

Prayer of Gratitude for Joy and Success:

Heavenly Father,

I come before you today with a heart brimming with gratitude and humility. You have blessed me with moments of joy and success, and I recognize that these are gifts from your abundant love.

Thank you for the joy that fills my heart when I achieve my goals, when I witness the beauty of creation, and when I am surrounded by the love of family and friends. Your blessings are beyond measure, and I am grateful for each one.

As I reflect on these moments of joy and success, I surrender any sense of pride or self-sufficiency. I acknowledge that it is your guidance, grace, and providence that have brought me to this place of abundance.

Help me to use these moments as opportunities to glorify you and to be of service to others. May my joy be a light that shines your love into the world, and may my success be a testament to your faithfulness and grace.

In times of joy and success, I surrender my desire for more and instead embrace contentment and gratitude. I trust in your plan for my life, knowing that you have already prepared a path filled with purpose and fulfillment.

May my life be a living prayer of gratitude and surrender, a reflection of your love and grace. With a heart full of thanksgiving, I offer this prayer in your holy name. Amen.

Meditation for Surrender in Moments of Joy and Success:

1. Find a Quiet Space: Begin by finding a quiet and peaceful space where you can sit or lie down comfortably.

2. Breathe Deeply: Close your eyes and take a few deep breaths. Inhale slowly and deeply, and then exhale slowly, releasing any tension or stress with each breath.

3.Reflect on Moments of Joy: Think about moments in your life when you have experienced pure joy and success. These could be personal achievements, milestones, or simply moments of happiness and contentment.

4. Express Gratitude: As you reflect on these moments, express your gratitude to God for each one. Offer specific thanks for the people, circumstances, and opportunities that have brought you joy and success.

5. Visualize Surrender: Imagine yourself holding these moments of joy and success in your hands, like precious gifts. Then, visualize yourself releasing them into the loving and capable hands of God. See them floating upward, becoming part of a beautiful tapestry of grace.

6. Surrender Your Desire for Control: Recognize that, in moments of joy and success, it's easy to feel a sense of control and ownership. Surrender this desire for control to God, acknowledging that He is the ultimate source of your blessings.

7. Embrace Humility: Embrace humility as you acknowledge that your achievements are not solely the result of your efforts but are also gifts from a loving Creator. Let go of any pride or ego associated with your success.

8. Trust in God's Plan: Surrender your desire for more and trust in God's plan for your life. Know that He has a purpose and a path for you, one that may lead to even greater joy and success.

9. Open Your Heart to Service: In moments of joy and success, commit to using your blessings to serve others and to be a source of light and love in the world. Surrender any selfish ambitions and replace them with a desire to make a positive impact.

10. Close in Prayer: Conclude your meditation with a prayer of

surrender and dedication. Offer your life, your moments of joy, and your successes to God's loving care. Ask for guidance in using these blessings for His glory and the well-being of others.

Remember that moments of joy and success are opportunities not only for gratitude but also for surrender. By acknowledging that these blessings come from God and surrendering your desire for control, you can find even deeper meaning and purpose in your life's journey. Surrendering in moments of joy and success allows you to become a conduit of God's love and grace, touching the lives of others and bringing greater fulfillment to your own.

Surrender can enhance the experience of Blessings and Happiness

Surrender is a profound and transformative practice that can enhance the experience of blessings and happiness in our lives. It involves letting go of our need to control, accepting what is, and placing our trust in a higher power, whether you call that power God, the universe, or something else. Here's how surrender can enhance the experience of blessings and happiness:

1. Deepens Gratitude: Surrender helps us appreciate and be truly grateful for the blessings we receive. When we surrender control and acknowledge that we aren't entitled to anything, we begin to see every blessing as a gift. This deepens our gratitude, making us more aware of the beauty and abundance around us.

2. Reduces Anxiety: Surrendering allows us to release the burdens of worry and anxiety. Instead of constantly striving

and fretting about the future, we trust that things will work out as they should. This reduction in anxiety opens up space for happiness to flourish.

3. Fosters Contentment: Surrender teaches us to be content with what we have rather than constantly chasing more. When we accept our current circumstances and trust that they are part of a greater plan, we find contentment in the present moment, which is a key ingredient of happiness.

4. Strengthens Resilience: Surrender is not passive resignation but an act of trust and faith. It strengthens our resilience because it teaches us to bounce back from setbacks and adversity. We realize that even in challenging times, there is a higher purpose, and this understanding makes us more resilient in the face of difficulties.

5. Enhances Mindfulness: Surrender encourages us to live in the present moment. When we stop dwelling on past regrets or worrying about future uncertainties, we become more mindful of the here and now. This heightened awareness of the present allows us to savor the blessings and moments of happiness as they occur.

6. Nurtures Trust: Surrender involves trusting in a higher power or divine plan. This trust provides a sense of security and comfort. It allows us to let go of the need to control every aspect of our lives and, in turn, fosters a sense of ease and happiness.

7. Promotes Positive Relationships: Surrender can also enhance our relationships. When we surrender our ego and the need to

be right or in control, we become more open, empathetic, and compassionate. This leads to more harmonious and fulfilling connections with others, contributing to our overall happiness.

8. Provides Perspective: Surrender offers a broader perspective on life. It reminds us that our happiness is not solely dependent on external circumstances but is also influenced by our inner state of mind. This perspective shift can lead to a more enduring and profound sense of happiness.

9. Encourages Flow: Surrender allows us to flow with the rhythms of life. We become less resistant to change and more adaptable. This flow state aligns us with the natural order of things, where happiness often resides.

10.Cultivates Spiritual Growth: Surrender is a deeply spiritual practice that can lead to personal growth and a greater sense of purpose. As we surrender our will to a higher power, we become more attuned to our spiritual journey, which often brings profound happiness and fulfillment.

Incorporating surrender into your life doesn't mean giving up or resigning yourself to fate. It's about finding a balance between effort and letting go, between pursuing your goals and trusting in the unfolding of life. When you surrender, you open yourself up to a deeper and more meaningful experience of blessings and happiness that transcends external circumstances and emanates from within. It's a path to greater peace, contentment, and joy.

Stories of thanksgiving and surrender from various life milestones:

Story 1: A Wedding Blessing

Jane and Mark had been planning their dream wedding for over a year. They wanted everything to be perfect, from the venue to the flowers and the guest list. However, as their big day approached, they faced a sudden and unexpected challenge—a hurricane was forecasted to hit their wedding location.

Despite their best efforts, they couldn't change the weather. Faced with the possibility of their carefully planned day being ruined, Jane and Mark made a decision. They chose to surrender their attachment to perfection and control and instead focus on what truly mattered—their love for each other and the support of their friends and family.

On their wedding day, the storm arrived as predicted, but so did their loved ones. The ceremony was moved indoors, and it turned out to be an intimate and heartwarming affair. The weather may not have been perfect, but the love in the room was undeniable. Jane and Mark realized that sometimes, surrendering control can lead to unexpected blessings, and they were filled with gratitude for their unforgettable wedding day.

Story 2: A Career Transition

David had spent over a decade working in a high-stress corporate job. Although he had achieved financial success, he felt unfulfilled and burnt out. One day, he decided to make a radical career change and pursue his passion for music.

The transition wasn't easy. David faced financial uncertainty and the fear of the unknown. However, he surrendered his attachment to his previous career and trusted that he was following his true calling. He started a small music school and began teaching children to play the piano.

Over the years, David's music school grew, and he found deep satisfaction in sharing his love for music with others. He realized that surrendering his old career had allowed him to discover his true purpose. With gratitude in his heart, he looked back on his journey with thanksgiving, knowing that the change had led to a more fulfilling life.

Story 3: Welcoming a New Life

Linda and Robert had been trying to conceive a child for years without success. They had undergone fertility treatments and endured numerous disappointments. It was a painful and emotionally draining journey, and they began to lose hope.

One day, as they sat together in a quiet moment of reflection, they decided to surrender their desperation and need for control. They recognized that there was only so much they could do, and the rest was beyond their power. They turned to prayer and entrusted their dreams of parenthood to a higher power.

Not long after, Linda and Robert received the joyful news that they were expecting a baby. The pregnancy was a time of deep gratitude and surrender. They realized that sometimes, despite our best efforts, we must surrender to the timing of life. When their daughter was born, they named her Grace, a constant reminder of the blessings that come when we let go and trust in the journey.

Story 4: A Health Transformation

Karen had struggled with her weight and overall health for
most of her adult life. She had tried various diets and exercise
programs without lasting success. One day, she decided to surrender her obsession with quick fixes and drastic measures. She
embraced a holistic approach to health, focusing on nourishing
her body and mind.

Karen began practicing yoga, meditating, and making mindful
choices about her diet. Over time, her health began to improve.
She lost weight, gained energy, and felt a sense of well-being she
had never experienced before. She surrendered her attachment
to a specific number on the scale and focused on the journey of
self-care.

With thanksgiving in her heart, Karen realized that true health
wasn't about perfection but about balance and self-compassion.
She was grateful for the transformation in her life, which had
come through surrendering her old habits and embracing a
healthier way of living.

These stories remind us that surrendering control and trusting
in a higher power can lead to unexpected blessings and moments
of gratitude. Whether it's a wedding, a career change, the
arrival of a child, or a health transformation, surrendering our
attachment to outcomes can open the door to a deeper sense of
fulfillment and thanksgiving in life's various milestones.

17

Surrender in Decision-Making

Seeking God's guidance through surrender when faced with life-altering decisions is a deeply spiritual and personal journey. Practical advice to help you navigate this process:

1. Cultivate a Relationship with God:
   - Building a strong foundation of faith and spirituality is essential. Regularly engage in prayer, meditation, and reading spiritual texts. Strengthen your connection with God so that seeking His guidance becomes a natural part of your life.

2. Understand God's Character:
   - Reflect on God's attributes, such as love, wisdom, and faithfulness. Know that He desires your well-being and has a plan for your life. Trust in His goodness and sovereignty.

3. Pray for Wisdom and Clarity:
   - When faced with a life-altering decision, pray for wisdom, clarity, and discernment. Ask God to reveal His will to you and guide your steps. Pour out your thoughts and emotions in prayer,

honestly sharing your hopes and fears.

4. Seek Counsel:

- Consult with trusted spiritual mentors, clergy, or wise individuals who share your faith. Their guidance and perspective can provide valuable insights as you make decisions.

5. Use Scripture as a Guide:

- Search for relevant passages in your religious texts that relate to your decision. Scripture can offer guidance and wisdom that align with your faith and values.

6. Listen to Your Inner Voice:

- Pay attention to your intuition and the inner prompting of the Holy Spirit. Sometimes, God communicates His guidance through a still, small voice within you.

7. Surrender Your Desires:

- Practice surrender by letting go of preconceived notions and desires. Be open to God's plan, even if it differs from what you initially expected or wanted.

8. Fast and Reflect:

- Consider fasting as a way to draw closer to God and seek His guidance. Fasting can create a focused, spiritually receptive state of mind. During this time, reflect on your decision and seek God's direction.

9. Give It Time:

- Avoid rushing important decisions. Give yourself time to pray, reflect, and seek guidance from others. Trust that God's timing is perfect and that clarity will come in His time.

10. Use a Decision-Making Framework:

   - Some faith traditions have specific decision-making frameworks or discernment practices. Explore these resources to help you make decisions that align with your beliefs.

11. Practice Gratitude and Trust:

   - While waiting for guidance, practice gratitude for the blessings you have received and trust in God's plan. Gratitude can shift your focus from uncertainty to the present moment.

12. Take Small Steps:

   - Sometimes, God's guidance becomes clearer as you take small steps in a particular direction. Trust that each step is leading you toward His plan.

13. Be Open to Detours:

   - God's guidance may lead you on unexpected paths or require detours from your original plan. Embrace these changes with faith and an open heart.

14. Accept That It May Not Be Easy:

   - Seeking God's guidance through surrender doesn't guarantee that decisions will be easy or without challenges. Accept that you may face obstacles but trust that God is with you throughout the journey.

15. Continuously Surrender and Trust:

   - Surrender is not a one-time act; it's a continuous process. As you make decisions and face their consequences, keep surrendering your desires and outcomes to God's care. Trust that He is guiding you, even in times of uncertainty.

Remember that seeking God's guidance through surrender is a personal and evolving practice. It's okay to have doubts and questions along the way. Ultimately, the journey of faith involves trust, surrender, and a willingness to align your decisions with your beliefs and values as you seek God's divine guidance in life-altering decisions.

Prayers for discernment and wisdom:

Prayer for Discernment:

Heavenly Father,

I come before you seeking discernment and clarity in the decisions I must make. I know that your wisdom surpasses all understanding, and I trust in your guidance.

Please grant me the discernment to recognize the right path amidst the choices before me. Open my heart and mind to your voice and the nudges of the Holy Spirit. Help me to see beyond the surface and discern the deeper truths.

In moments of uncertainty, when I'm unsure of which way to turn, be my guiding light. Illuminate the path that aligns with your will, even if it differs from my own desires.

Grant me patience as I seek your discernment, knowing that your timing is perfect. May I move forward with confidence, knowing that I have sought your wisdom in every decision.

I surrender my own understanding and lean on your divine wisdom. With faith and trust, I seek your discernment, knowing that you will lead me along the path of righteousness.

In the name of your Son, Jesus Christ, I pray. Amen.

Prayer for Wisdom:

Eternal God,

I humbly come before you, recognizing my need for wisdom in every aspect of my life. Your Word tells me that if I lack wisdom, I can ask, and you will generously provide it.

Today, I ask for your wisdom, which is pure, peace-loving, considerate, full of mercy and good fruit. Grant me the wisdom to make choices that honor you and bring goodness into the world.

Help me to discern right from wrong, to see beyond the immediate, and to understand the consequences of my decisions. May your wisdom guide my thoughts, words, and actions.

In moments of uncertainty, when I'm faced with difficult choices, may your wisdom be my anchor and compass. Let it shine as a light upon my path, leading me to choices that reflect your love and grace.

I surrender my limited understanding and trust in your infinite wisdom. Grant me the discernment to apply your wisdom in my daily life, so that I may walk in the path of righteousness and be a source of blessing to others.

In the name of your Son, Jesus Christ, I pray. Amen.

These prayers for discernment and wisdom are tools to help you seek divine guidance in your life's decisions. Feel free to personalize them and make them your own as you engage in a conversation with your higher power, seeking wisdom and discernment for the choices that lie ahead.

Surrendering in relationships is an ongoing practice that involves humility, empathy, and a willingness to let go of ego-driven behaviors. It can lead to deeper connections, improved communication, and more fulfilling interactions with your family, friends, and romantic partners. Remember that surrender is a two-way street, and both parties can benefit from the practice.

18

Surrender in Faith and Spirituality

Prayers for reconciliation, forgiveness, and healing:

Prayer for Reconciliation:

Heavenly Father,

I come before you with a heavy heart, burdened by broken relationships and the pain of separation. I long for reconciliation, for healing the wounds that have driven those I care about apart.

Lord, you are the God of reconciliation, the mender of broken bonds. I surrender these fractured relationships to your divine care. Soften hearts that have grown hardened, and help us find a path back to one another.

Grant us the humility to acknowledge our faults and the grace to forgive. Fill us with love, empathy, and understanding. Guide our words and actions as we seek reconciliation, and let your peace prevail over our conflicts.

In your name, I pray for the mending of relationships, the restoration of love, and the reconciliation of hearts. May your divine grace lead us back to one another, stronger and more united than before. Amen.

Prayer for Forgiveness:

Merciful God,

I stand before you in need of your forgiveness, both for the wrongs I have committed and for the forgiveness I seek to offer others. I surrender my pride and ego, acknowledging my imperfections and mistakes.

Lord, you are the model of forgiveness, offering your grace even to those who have wronged you. Teach me to forgive as you forgive, to release the burden of resentment, and to let go of past hurts.

Help me to understand that forgiveness is not condoning wrong-doing but choosing to let go of the poison of unforgiveness. Fill my heart with compassion and empathy for those who have hurt me, and grant me the strength to extend the gift of forgiveness.

I surrender my need for revenge or retribution and instead choose the path of forgiveness, which leads to healing and reconciliation. May your grace enable me to forgive and be forgiven, and may it bring peace to my heart and the hearts of those I have wronged. In your name, I pray. Amen.

Prayer for Healing:

Healing God,

I come before you, recognizing the pain and suffering in my life and the lives of those I love. I surrender these wounds to your loving care, knowing that you are the ultimate source of healing and restoration.

Lord, you are the great Physician, capable of mending not only physical ailments but also the brokenness of our hearts and souls. I ask for your healing touch to mend what is broken, to soothe what is wounded, and to restore what is lost.

Grant us the strength to endure the process of healing, which often requires patience and faith. May your healing grace flow through us, bringing comfort, peace, and strength.

I surrender my doubts and fears about the future and trust in your divine plan for my wholeness and well-being. In your name, I pray for healing in every aspect of my life—physically, emotionally, and spiritually. May your restorative power bring renewal and hope. Amen.

These prayers for reconciliation, forgiveness, and healing are tools to help you seek divine assistance and find peace and resolution in challenging times. Feel free to personalize these prayers to align with your own intentions and needs.

Deepening one's faith through Surrender

Deepening one's faith through surrender is a profound spiritual journey that involves letting go of control and trusting in a higher power. Here are some insights into how surrender can lead to a deeper faith:

1. Trust in Divine Plan: Surrender begins with the acknowledgment that there is a divine plan or purpose for our lives. Deepening faith involves trusting that this plan is for our ultimate good, even when we can't see the bigger picture.

2. Letting Go of Ego: Surrendering requires us to let go of our ego's need to be in control. It's recognizing that our understanding is limited, and there is a higher wisdom at play. This humility fosters a deeper faith in something greater than ourselves.

3. Prayer and Meditation: Surrendering often involves a regular practice of prayer and meditation. These practices create moments of connection with the divine and allow us to release our worries and desires, deepening our faith in the power of prayer.

4. Surrendering Worry and Anxiety: Faith and worry are often at odds. Surrendering our anxieties and worries to a higher power can lead to a more peaceful and faith-filled life. It's an ongoing process of relinquishing our fears and trusting that we will be taken care of.

5. Accepting the Unpredictable: Life is unpredictable, and surrendering to this unpredictability can deepen faith. When we accept that we can't control every aspect of our lives, we rely on faith to navigate the unknown.

6. Seeing Blessings in Challenges: Surrender helps us see

blessings in challenges. It's understanding that even in difficult times, there is a purpose and a lesson to be learned. This perspective shift deepens our faith in the goodness of the divine.

7. Living in the Present: Surrender encourages us to live in the present moment rather than constantly striving for the future. This presence allows us to experience the divine in the here and now, deepening our faith in the sacredness of everyday life.

8. Seeking Guidance: Surrender doesn't mean we stop seeking guidance from religious or spiritual sources. In fact, it often leads us to seek more profound spiritual guidance and wisdom, which strengthens our faith.

9. Experiencing Grace: Surrender often leads to experiences of grace—those moments when we feel a profound connection with the divine. These moments deepen our faith and serve as reminders of the presence of the sacred in our lives.

10. Embracing Mystery: Faith involves an element of mystery. Surrender allows us to embrace this mystery and find beauty and wonder in the unknown. It's an acknowledgment that not everything can be explained or understood, which deepens our faith in the divine mystery.

11. Loving and Serving Others: Surrender often leads to a desire to love and serve others selflessly. This expression of faith through acts of kindness and compassion can deepen our connection to the divine and strengthen our faith in the power of love.

In essence, deepening one's faith through surrender is a transformative process of letting go, trusting, and finding meaning and purpose in the journey. It's a journey that can lead to a profound and enduring connection with the divine and a richer, more fulfilling spiritual life.

19

Final Prayer of Surrender

Heavenly Father,

As I come before you one final time in these pages, I humbly offer a prayer of surrender. I surrender my desires, my plans, and my will to your divine wisdom and love.

Lord, I trust that your plan for my life is greater than anything I can imagine. I release my need for control and embrace your sovereignty. Help me to surrender daily, to find strength in humility, and to walk in the light of your guidance.

In moments of uncertainty, grant me the faith to trust in your goodness. In times of sorrow, fill my heart with your comfort. And in times of joy, help me to remember that all blessings come from you.

I surrender my fears and anxieties, knowing that you are my refuge and strength. I surrender my desires and dreams, knowing that your plan is perfect and purposeful.

May this act of surrender be a testament to my faith in you. May it be a source of peace and serenity in my life. May it be a reminder that in letting go, I find my true self in you.

I surrender, Lord, not out of weakness, but out of strength. I surrender, not as a defeat, but as a victory over my own ego. I surrender, not because I have to, but because I choose to, knowing that in surrendering, I find my true freedom in you.

Thank you, Lord, for your boundless love and grace. May your presence be with me on this journey of surrender, guiding me every step of the way.

In your holy and loving name, I pray. Amen.

20

Conclusion

In conclusion, the journey of surrender, as explored in this book, is a path of profound spiritual growth and connection with the divine. It's about letting go of our need for control, trusting in a higher power, and finding peace in the midst of life's uncertainties.

Throughout these pages, we have delved into the power of surrender in various aspects of life—relationships, challenges, decisions, and moments of joy. We've discovered that surrender is not a sign of weakness but a source of strength, resilience, and deep inner peace.

In times of hardship, grief, and uncertainty, we have learned to turn to surrender as a refuge, a place where we release our burdens and find solace in the loving embrace of a higher power. Through powerful prayers and reflections, we have seen how surrender can transform our struggles into opportunities for growth and healing.

We have explored the concept of surrender in the context of faith, understanding that it is a fundamental aspect of a deep and abiding relationship with the divine. Surrender is the bridge that connects us to the sacred, the pathway to trust, and the gateway to grace.

In moments of joy and success, we have witnessed the beauty of surrender as a way to express gratitude and deepen our connection with the divine. It's a reminder that even in times of abundance, we remain humble and thankful for the blessings we receive.

We have also tackled common misconceptions about surrender, clarifying that it does not mean giving up or resigning ourselves to fate. Instead, surrender is an act of faith, a surrender of our ego-driven desires to a higher and wiser power.

As we conclude this book, let us remember that surrender is an ongoing journey—a journey that invites us to release, trust, and embrace the divine will in every aspect of our lives. It's an invitation to surrender not only in times of need but in every occasion, recognizing that the divine is always with us, guiding us, and loving us.

May the prayers, reflections, and guidance in this book serve as companions on your own journey of surrender. May they inspire you to cultivate a deeper faith, find peace in the midst of life's challenges, and experience the transformative power of surrender in your life.

May your surrender to God's will lead you to a life filled with purpose, joy, and a profound sense of connection to the divine. In the spirit of surrender, may you find the peace that surpasses all understanding.

With heartfelt blessings and love,

[Your Name]

Made in United States
Troutdale, OR
03/12/2024

18411968R00056